rediscover

NATURAL WORLD

KANGAROO

HABITATS • LIFE CYCLES • FOOD CHAINS • THREATS

Malcolm Penny

W
HODDER
Wayland
an imprint of Hodder
Children's Books

WWF

Produced in Association with WWF-UK

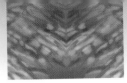

NATURAL WORLD

Black Rhino • Cheetah • Chimpanzee • Crocodile • Dolphin
Giant Panda • Giraffe • Golden Eagle • Gorilla • Great White Shark
Hippopotamus • Kangaroo • Koala • Leopard • Moose
Orangutan • Penguin • Polar Bear • Seal • Tiger • Wolf • Zebra

Produced for Hodder Wayland by
Monkey Puzzle Media Ltd
Gissing's Farm, Fressingfield
Suffolk IP21 5SH, UK

Produced in association with WWF-UK.
WWF-UK registered charity number
1081247. A company limited by guarantee
number 4016725. Panda device © 1986 WWF.
® WWF registered trademark owner.

The website addresses (URLs) included in this book
were valid at the time of going to press. However,
because of the nature of the Internet, it is possible
that some addresses may have changed, or sites may
have changed or closed down since publication.
While the authors and Publishers regret any
inconvenience this may cause the readers, no
responsibility for any such changes can be
accepted by either the author or the Publisher.

Cover: Face to face with a grey kangaroo.
Title page: Red kangaroo at full speed.
Contents page: An eastern grey kangaroo.
Index page: Eastern greys feeding in a cornfield.

Published in Great Britain in 2003 by Hodder Wayland,
an imprint of Hodder Children's Books
Text copyright © 2003 Hodder Wayland
Volume copyright © 2003 Hodder Wayland

This paperback edition published in 2004

Editor: Angela Wilkes
Series editor: Victoria Brooker
Designer: Sarah Crouch

British Library Cataloguing in Publication Data
Penny, Malcolm
  Kangaroo. - (Natural world)
  1.Kangaroos - Juvenile literature
  I.Title
  599.2'22

ISBN 0 7502 4246 9

Printed in China

Hodder Children's Books
A division of Hodder Headline Limited
338 Euston Road, London NW1 3BH

Picture acknowledgements
FLPA front cover Gerard Lacz, 1 Gerard Lacz, 6 David
Hosking, 10 J Finch, 12 Jurgen and Christine Sohns,
30 Tom and Pam Gardner, 31 Mark Newman, 33
Mark Newman, 34 Gerard Lacz, 37 Mark Newman,
38 David Hosking, 39 Eric Woods, 41 Mark Newman,
42 Tom and Pam Gardner, 44 top J Finch, 45 bottom
Mark Newman; *Nature Picture Library* 8 Warwick
Sloss, 9 Anup Shah, 13 John Cancalosi, 15 Ingo Arndt,
18 Dave Watts; *NHPA* 7 Gerard Lacz, 17 Martin
Harvey, 29 Patrick Fagot, 32 Martin Harvey, 35 Dave
Watts, 40 Daniel Zupanc, 43 ANT Photo library;
Oxford Scientific Films 16 Kathie Atkinson, 19, 20
Kathie Atkinson, 22 Des and Jen Bartlett/SAL, 23
Roger Brown, 25 Des and Jen Bartlett/SAL, 27 Kathie
Atkinson, 28 Kathie Atkinson, 36 Kathie Atkinson, 45
top Kathie Atkinson, 45 middle Kathie Atkinson, 48
Des and Jen Bartlett/SAL; *Science Photo Library* 3 Phil
Dotson, 11 Dale Boyer, 14 Art Wolfe, 24 Wayne
Lawler, 26 Tom McHugh, 44 middle Dale Boyer, 44
bottom Art Wolfe. Artwork by Michael Posen.

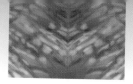

Contents

Meet the Kangaroo

Kangaroos are unmistakable. Their shape and the way they move cannot be confused with any other animal. There are several species of kangaroo, both large and small. Most of them live in Australia, but a few live in New Guinea.

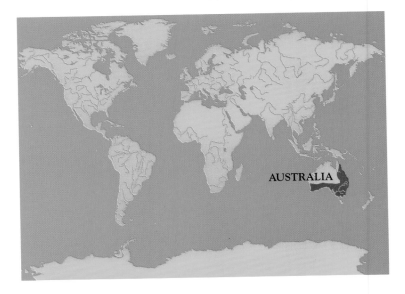

AUSTRALIA

▶ The red shading on this map shows where grey kangaroos live.

KANGAROO FACTS

The large kangaroos all have the scientific name *Macropus*, which means 'bigfoot'. The eastern grey kangaroo is known as *Macropus giganteus*, 'giant bigfoot', and the red kangaroo is *Macropus rufus*, 'red bigfoot'.

Grey kangaroos grow to 1.5 metres tall. The males weigh about 70 kilograms, and the females half as much. Red kangaroos grow to 1.6 metres tall, and weigh up to 90 kilograms. Antilopine kangaroos are similar in size to greys. Males reach 70 kilograms, but females are much smaller, weighing about 30 kilograms.

Kangaroos are marsupial mammals. This means that their babies are born before they are fully developed and finish developing inside pouches on their mothers' bellies. The babies are born so early that they would be unable to survive outside. Kangaroos are adaptable animals and live in a wide range of habitats.

▼ An eastern grey kangaroo.

Eyes and ears
Wide field of view.
Large, mobile ears

Teeth
Long jaws with specialised grass-eating teeth

Hands
Small forelegs with five claws

Legs
Powerful hind legs with two strong claws

Tail
Long heavy tail

The habitat of the eastern grey kangaroo

The eastern grey kangaroo originally lived in damp forests and woodlands in eastern Australia, though it ranged across the south as well. But when Europeans first arrived in Australia, around 1770, they built dams and dug wells to provide water for their farm animals. Since then, grey kangaroos have spread into parts of the region that used to be much drier. Some western greys live in the same area, but they prefer woodlands with smaller trees or scrub.

▼ An eastern grey kangaroo in its natural habitat.

The grey kangaroo's neighbours in the woodland include animals as unique as the kangaroos themselves, such as the spiny anteater, or echidna, and the duck-billed platypus. Many small kangaroos, such as potoroos and bettongs, live in the woods. They are mostly herbivores. There are also wombats, large burrowing marsupials rather like badgers, and marsupial mice. The birds in the woods include the kookaburra, a giant land-based kingfisher, and the tuneful butcher bird.

▲ Dingoes are attractive, intelligent dogs, but powerful hunters.

OUTSIDERS

These days Australia is home to many mammals brought in from other countries. The first to arrive was the dingo. It came with the Aborigines, probably from New Guinea, seven to ten thousand years ago. The dingo's main prey is rabbits, which were introduced by European settlers. In about 1845 settlers also brought foxes to Australia.

▶ Red kangaroos have to eat whatever they can find in the hot, dry Outback.

Kangaroo relatives

Kangaroos can live in many different habitats. The red kangaroo, the most common species, roams the dry, open plains. The antilopine kangaroo lives in hot, damp woodlands in the north. It looks like an antelope, with its slim build, long legs and smooth fur.

Middle-sized kangaroos are called wallaroos. These are smaller than other kangaroos and have short, strong legs. They live in hilly, rocky country and their hind feet have rough soles, giving them a good grip on the rocks.

Tree kangaroos look very different from other kangaroos. They have stocky front legs and much shorter back legs. They grip branches with their front claws and walk up trees, moving their back legs one at a time. No other kangaroos can do this.

Rat kangaroos are small, omnivorous kangaroos that live in the woods and feed by day. They gather bundles of ferns and grasses in their mouths to use as nesting material. They then kick the bundles behind them and pick them up with their tails, so they can carry them to where they will nest.

► A tree kangaroo's strong claws enable it to climb up tree trunks easily.

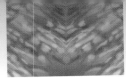

A Kangaroo is Born

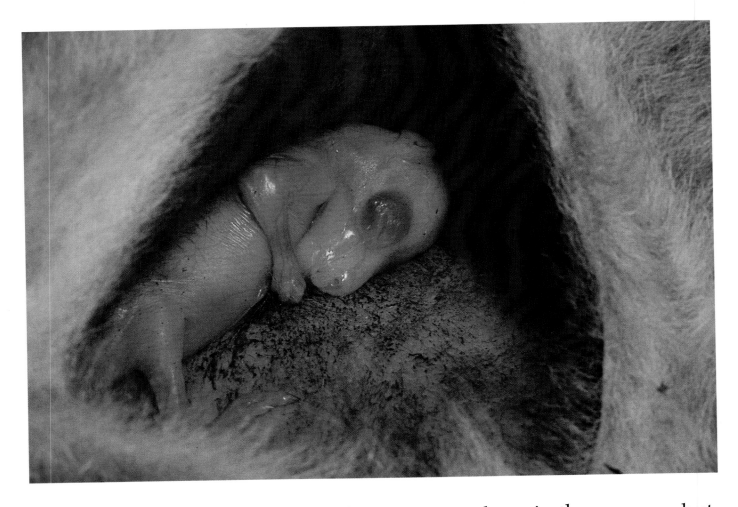

▲ This tiny grey kangaroo is only a few days old. Its mother's pouch will be its home for the next nine months.

Most grey kangaroos are born in the summer, but they are sometimes born at other times, if there is plenty of food. A few days before a female kangaroo gives birth, she opens her pouch with her front paws and carefully licks the inside. She does this until an hour before the baby is born. She then sits in a special birthing position, leaning back on her tail and the heels of her hind feet.

◀ A young red joey watches its mother feeding from the comfort of her pouch.

The newborn kangaroo is less than two centimetres long and weighs less than three-quarters of a gram. For about ten seconds it lies still. Then it starts to climb up towards its mother's pouch. Its front legs have tiny claws, which it uses to grasp its mother's fur. When it crawls into the pouch it grips one of its mother's four teats in its mouth. It will stay attached to the teat for about four months, warm and protected, with a steady supply of milk.

Although the baby kangaroo is at a very early stage of development, two important senses are working already. It can tell the difference between up and down, so that it can climb upwards to the pouch. It also has a good sense of smell, to help it find one of its mother's teats.

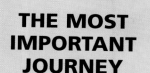

THE MOST IMPORTANT JOURNEY

The journey from the birth canal to the rim of the pouch is about 20 centimetres, and it takes the baby kangaroo about three minutes. It is the most important journey it ever makes in its life.

First days

The baby kangaroo is called a joey. While the joey is living in its mother's pouch, she cleans the pouch out regularly. The tiny joey is held safely in the pouch by strong muscles round the top.

The mother kangaroo has other work to do. Unless this is her first baby, she has another baby that has already left her pouch. This active little 'joey at foot' keeps her very busy. She has to groom it and play with it, and she also has to feed it. The joey at foot feeds from one of the teats not being used by the tiny joey. The mother kangaroo has to produce two different types of milk. The joey in the pouch needs fatty milk, while the joey at foot needs milk rich in proteins. The tiny joey drinks very little, but the joey at foot weighs up to four kilograms and needs far more.

▼ After about six months, the joey in the pouch starts popping its head out to look around. If its mother is grazing, this gives the joey the chance to nibble its first blades of grass.

SAFETY POUCHES

All kangaroo pouches open upwards, towards the mother's front. Most other marsupials, such as koalas and possums, have pouches that open to the back. The pouch openings of all marsupials are held shut by strong muscles, keeping the babies safely tucked inside.

Grey kangaroo joeys grow more slowly in the pouch than other species and spend longer there. A red kangaroo joey first leaves its mother's pouch after about six months. Eastern greys leave after about nine months.

▲ A young koala clings to its mother's back until it is old enough to climb trees by itself.

Leaving the pouch

When the joey first leaves the pouch, it is very wobbly on its feet, and often climbs straight back in again. It dives in headfirst and turns a somersault so its head pokes out of the top. Later, it will come back to the pouch to suckle, sometimes just putting its head in for comfort.

But one day, when the joey is about ten months old and tries to climb inside its mother's pouch, she leans forward and relaxes her pouch muscles so that it falls out. It soon realises that it is no longer welcome to ride in there.

▲ A female red kangaroo, sometimes called a 'blue flier' because of her grey coat, suckling a large joey.

A grey joey feeds from its mother until it is eighteen months old. Red kangaroos are weaned at about a year old, and antilopine kangaroos about a month later. By now, male eastern grey joeys and red joeys weigh about 17 kilograms. Female grey joeys weigh about 12 kilograms and female reds about 14 kilograms.

▶ A young eastern grey joey has a lot to learn when it comes out of the pouch.

EMERGENCY!

When a mother kangaroo is in danger, she opens her pouch and drops her joey out, leaving it to look after itself. This means that she can escape to safety more quickly, but the joey often dies. At least the mother will survive and carry on to have more babies.

Neighbours in the forest

When the joey has left the pouch it becomes more independent, but it still follows its mother about and rests with her when they are not feeding. If the joey is distressed, it bleats loudly to its mother. At the first sign of danger, it scurries back to her and they hop to safety together.

As the joey becomes more confident it spends most of its time exploring its surroundings. It also meets its neighbours. Many of them are small marsupials, such as potoroos and bettongs, which live in the dense woodland undergrowth.

▲ An eastern grey joey feeds where its mother feeds, copying her and learning what is good to eat.

Most of the joey's neighbours are no threat. Some of them are even helpful. Two birds, the magpie lark and the willie wagtail, are often seen near kangaroos. Magpie larks pick parasites from their fur, while wagtails snap up insects that the kangaroos disturb, some of which are harmful.

▼ A willie wagtail uses a kangaroo as a look-out post as it watches for insects.

MARSUPIAL CATS AND MICE

The woodlands are the home of an unusual family of marsupials called the dasyures. Some look like mice and others like cats. Unlike other marsupials, these animals are carnivorous. The little northern native cat hunts lizards and insects. The eastern native cat hunts birds.

Unusual neighbours

Two of the grey kangaroo's neighbours are totally unique. The echidna and the duck-billed platypus are monotremes, a type of mammal with an unusual way of breeding. Unlike other mammals, they lay soft-shelled eggs, which hatch after ten days. Young echidnas grow up in their mother's pouch, like marsupials. Young platypuses live with their mother for three or four months in a breeding burrow.

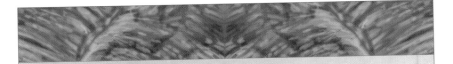

IT CAN'T BE TRUE!

When the first stuffed platypus was brought to England in about 1798, nobody believed that it was a real animal. They thought that a taxidermist had stitched a duck's beak on to the body of a mammal. Even when they knew it was real, people thought it was probably a reptile. It was 1973 before scientists proved that monotremes are warm-blooded, like other mammals.

▼ With duck feet as well as a duck bill, the platypus was a great surprise to the first Europeans who saw one.

Monotremes have fur, milk glands and warm blood, like other mammals. But unlike other mammals, the milk glands have no teats. The babies lick milk from their mother's belly instead.

▲ Echidnas feed mainly on ants, which they lick up with their long, sticky tongues.

Monotremes are also the only mammals, apart from some shrews, that produce poison. A male platypus can erect a sharp hollow spur on each ankle. When cornered, the platypus kicks out at an enemy and poison runs through the spur and into the wound. This is very painful to a human, and can kill a dog. Male echidnas have spurs and poison glands, but they do not work. Perhaps they are left over from some time in the past when the echidna had to defend itself against a predator that is now extinct.

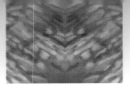

Choosing Food

▲ Grey kangaroos come out to feed in the evening light, after resting in the woods all day.

The grey kangaroo's favourite foods are the fresh grasses that grow in clearings and round the edge of woodland, and tender plants from the woodland floor. It also likes young leaves from bushes and shrubs. After good winter rains there is plenty of food and greys do not have to travel far to find enough to eat. If the rains are not good, they have to search for food, making do with any older grasses and leaves they can find. These are tough to chew and hard to digest.

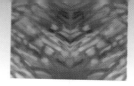

Red kangaroos do not have such a wide choice of food, as most of them live in the dry, open Outback. They still choose young grass and fresh plants when they can find them, but they can manage well on desert shrubs such as saltbush and bluebush, or old, dry grass.

Like all plant-eating animals, kangaroos digest their food with the help of bacteria in their gut. This process is called fermentation. Mammals cannot digest cellulose, the substance that forms plant cell walls, but the bacteria in their gut can.

KANGAROO FOOD CHAIN

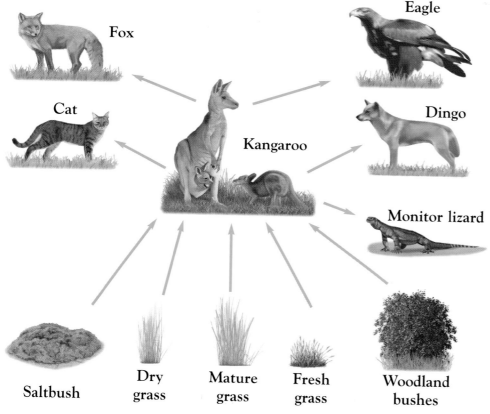

Fox

Cat

Eagle

Dingo

Kangaroo

Monitor lizard

Saltbush

Dry grass

Mature grass

Fresh grass

Woodland bushes

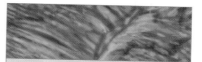

INEDIBLE PLANTS GROW BEST

It is not always easy to guess what kangaroos eat by looking at the vegetation around them. Some plants taste bad and others are poisonous. After kangaroos have been feeding in one place for a while, these might be the only plants left. Until the next good rains, the kangaroos might be hopping around among plenty of plants, yet have nothing to eat.

New pastures

Before Europeans arrived in Australia, travelling to find food was no problem for kangaroos. But farmers built long fences to protect their cattle against dingoes and the kangaroos could not jump over the fences. A continuous fence, stretching for 600 kilometres, was built all the way around New South Wales. Now that dingoes have become quite rare in Australia, farmers have stopped mending and building fences, so kangaroos are once again free to travel where they like, in search of food.

▲ At home on the plains: red kangaroos at full speed.

Many farmers think of kangaroos as a pest that steals the pastures planted for their herds. In fact, kangaroos eat far less than sheep or goats. A medium-sized grey kangaroo needs 540 grams of food a day. By comparison, a sheep needs 1130 grams of food a day, and a goat 1020 grams.

In dry weather, all kangaroos take longer to digest their food. They keep it in their gut for as long as possible to extract every last drop of moisture from it. Finding water is a serious problem during a drought.

▼ The stony desert may look barren, but it is full of food for a red kangaroo.

TEMPTATION

Kangaroos have fed on the native grasses and small plants in the Australian bush for millions of years, but these plants were not suitable for the livestock that Europeans brought with them. When farmers planted pastures for their animals, the kangaroos were naturally tempted by this rich new food supply.

Keeping cool, saving water

Grey kangaroos, which live in damp, shady places, are less careful with water than reds, which live in dry places. Greys have to drink three times as often as reds, and in hot weather they lose water very quickly. Red kangaroos only look for water about every five days. This is because hopping from place to place makes them hot and they have to use water to cool down. It is better to lie still in the cool shade.

▼ These red kangaroos are on a rare visit to a waterhole. The female is on the left, showing the difference in size between the sexes.

Like many other mammals, such as dogs, kangaroos keep cool mainly by panting. The skin inside a kangaroo's nose contains a lot of blood vessels. As the kangaroo's damp breath passes quickly over them, the moisture evaporates, cooling the blood. When a red kangaroo is hot, it pants up to 300 times per minute. Kangaroos cool down by sweating too, but they also have a third method that is totally unique: arm-licking. They spread water from glands in their noses on to their forearms, where it cools a dense network of blood vessels just below the skin.

▲ As if rolling up its sleeves, a red kangaroo licks its forearms to cool down.

A LIFE WITHOUT WATER

Spectacled hare wallabies are small kangaroos that live on Barrow Island off the coast of Western Australia. They never drink water, even when it rains on their dry island home. They obtain all the moisture they need from the food that they eat.

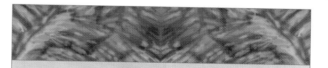

Growing Up

The young grey kangaroo learns to recognise its mother while it is still very small, so that it does not lose her if the group scatters in alarm. The mother and her joey feed close together, away from the others.

◀ Play-fighting with his mother helps a joey to learn fighting skills. The mother keeps her head well out of the way of the joey's claws.

As it grows bigger, the joey wanders away, but it dare not go very far. It needs to see animals that it knows. At first, these are its mother and any of her babies that are still with her. It also meets other families that live nearby. Family groups may stay together in the same place for many years and get to know each other really well.

Being near its friends helps to keep the young kangaroo safe from predators. Like most animals, kangaroos are safer in a group, because there are more pairs of eyes watching out for danger.

▲ A large male eastern grey has plenty to eat after good spring rains.

An important part of growing up, especially for a young male, is play-fighting with his mother. She boxes with her son, so that he learns the moves used in kangaroo fights. These skills will help him later on in life.

A kangaroo mob

During the day, grey kangaroos rest and feed in the woodlands, but they have to come out at night to find grass. Families often feed together in a large group known as a mob. Where there is plenty of food and little danger from predators, a mob of greys might have up to 80 members.

A mother kangaroo and her young feed in a home range of about 20 hectares, which they share with up to ten other females and their young. These groups live together peacefully, as all the kangaroos have known each other since they were young. Towards dawn, male grey kangaroos often prowl from one family group to another, probably to check whether any of the females are ready to mate.

▲ As the sun rises, a mob of greys finish their night's feeding and prepare to go and rest in the shady woodland.

▶ A male red kangaroo checks a female. Her large joey will soon leave the pouch for the last time.

The mob does not really have leaders, though older females sometimes play a leading role. When more than one family wants to feed or rest in a particular place, the leading female and her young move in without argument. Males have a less peaceful life. Because a leading male can mate with any female, other adult males often challenge him. Fighting is common, especially during the breeding season, but there are ways to avoid it.

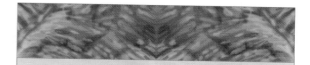

A PEACEFUL LIFE

Scientists studying social animals have found that living in small groups is better than living in large crowds. This is because members of a small group spend less time and energy dealing with strangers, so there is less risk of quarrelling and fighting. This is true for kangaroos and perhaps for people too.

Communications

Kangaroos hardly ever use their voices. Joeys bleat like lambs when they are alarmed, and their mothers call back, making soft clucking noises. Male kangaroos also cluck softly, during courtship. Kangaroos mainly communicate by sign-language. When two adults meet, they often greet each other by touching noses and sniffing. The smaller adult might then crouch close to the ground, with its head trembling, to show that it means no harm.

Groups of kangaroos are usually peaceful, but sometimes there are disagreements. Perhaps two families want to rest in the same place during the day, or two males want the same female. Then the threats begin.

▲ A mother and her joey touch noses. This is the usual form of greeting between kangaroos.

▶ When the threats come to an end, the young grey male must know what to do next.

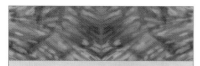

FIERCE FIGHTS

Fights between kangaroos are rare, but they can be very serious. Usually one animal backs down during the threat display and makes sharp clicking sounds like a small joey. It does this to avoid a fight, as both fighters run the risk of being injured.

First, the kangaroos sit up straight to make themselves look very tall. Then they stand on tiptoe, with one arm held out stiffly in front of them. They pull up tufts of grass to show they are angry, or pretend to fight with a nearby bush. Both males and females do this. Males then circle each other on stiff legs. If things become even more serious they lick their forearms, as if to cool themselves down. Joeys must learn to recognise these signs, to avoid being caught in a fight.

Fighting

Kangaroos fight in two different ways. Short, sharp scuffles are signs of a passing disagreement, but males competing for seniority take part in ritual fights, which last much longer. This is often called 'boxing', but instead of hitting each other, the two kangaroos try to scratch each other's face, ears and chest. They throw their heads back, to keep their faces out of range and often rest during the fight, to get their breath back before carrying on.

BOXING MATCHES

At one time people thought it entertaining to make kangaroos box with men. It may have looked funny, but if a kangaroo felt that it was losing it would kick out at the man. Many men were badly hurt as a result. This cruel practice has long been banned.

▲ Two greys of equal size fight, but the loser will hop away after this defensive kick.

◀ The smaller of these two red males knows he is losing the fight, so he prepares to kick his opponent.

A fight ends when one male is pushed to the ground or backs away. The kangaroo that started the fight usually wins. The loser sometimes sits back on his tail and kicks at his opponent. This is dangerous for the opponent, because a kangaroo's hind feet have sharp claws, and its back legs are very strong. Kangaroos kick in defence, to push their opponent out of range, but it can cause serious injury. When another animal is involved, such as a dog or a dingo that has attacked a joey, a kick can be fatal.

Adult Life

Kangaroos are the only large mammals that move by hopping with both their back feet together. After it takes off, a kangaroo swings its legs forward, ready to land. When it hits the ground, strong tendons in its heels, stretched like rubber bands, enable it to bounce up again. The kangaroo's heavy tail helps it to keep its balance, so that it does not fall forward on its face. A red kangaroo can keep up a steady speed of 25 kilometres per hour, making two hops per second, each about 4 metres long. As it speeds up, the hops become longer, until it reaches 40 kilometres per hour, a speed at which it can cruise for two kilometres. In an emergency, it can reach up to 70 kilometres per hour but only for a few hundred metres.

▼ Tail swinging and legs pumping, a red kangaroo hops at full speed.

▲ This western grey is walking slowly, using its 'fifth leg'.

Grey kangaroos are not as fast. Because they live in the woods, they do not have to travel such long distances in search of food as the desert-living reds.

FIVE LEGS

When kangaroos move at less than 6 kilometres per hour, they use their tail like a fifth leg, propping them up as they swing the hind legs forward. This is often called 'going on all fives'.

Finding a mate

Male eastern grey kangaroos are fully mature at about four years old. They leave their mother to live with a group of other young males, although they usually stay in the mob where they grew up. Females mature younger, at 18 months to two years, and stay close to their mothers. They can breed until they are about 12 years old. Female kangaroos breed for the first time when they are just over three years old, but males have to wait until they are five or even seven.

▶ A female eastern grey can breed at a younger age when there is plenty of food available.

▲ Female greys stay close to their mothers and their friends even when they are grown up.

EAT WELL, BREED YOUNG

Captive female grey kangaroos reach breeding age earlier than wild ones, at two years old instead of three. Scientists think that this is because they have plenty of food. In years when there is more food in the wild, the females are ready to breed younger than usual.

Red kangaroos breed all the year round, but the greys' main breeding season is usually from October to March. This can be longer when there is plenty of food. Antilopine kangaroos breed in March and April.

When a female is ready to breed, she gives off a distinctive scent. Males regularly check the scent of females in their area and follow one that is ready to mate. They fight amongst themselves to win the female and the biggest and strongest male usually wins. An eastern grey male needs to weigh about 70 kilograms before he has a chance of mating.

Threats

Kangaroos' lives changed enormously when humans came to Australia. The Aborigines, who were first to arrive, were expert hunters, and there are signs that they quickly wiped out some species of huge kangaroos that lived in those days. They also brought with them dingoes, which have become one of the kangaroo's few natural enemies. Others include eagles, snakes and monitor lizards.

▼ The Aborigines made drawings in caves of the animals they hunted, including kangaroos.

When Europeans arrived in Australia in the 1770s they caused even greater changes. They not only brought in predators, such as cats, dogs and foxes, but also sheep and cattle. These caused problems. Farmers shot kangaroos for eating the grass they had planted for their herds and for drinking the water they had provided for their cattle and sheep in the dry Outback.

Eventually, grey and red kangaroos spread into all the areas that the farmers provided with water and grass. As a result, red kangaroos are found deep in the Outback, and grey kangaroos far from the damp woodlands where they originally lived. The large kangaroos are more numerous today than they were when Europeans first arrived, and in some places they are treated as pests.

DANGER ON THE ROADS

Many country roads in the Outback are edged with grass, watered by the dew that collects on the roads at night. Kangaroos come to lick up the dew and eat the grass, and many are killed by cars and trucks every year. Most country drivers in Australia have 'roo-bars' on the front of their cars to protect them from collisions with kangaroos.

◀ 'Beware – Roos Crossing'. Accidents can be caused by kangaroos bounding across roads in the Outback.

Conservation

Although large kangaroos are more widespread and have increased in numbers since Europeans came to Australia, we know that they do not compete directly with sheep and cattle. They eat different kinds of grass and less of it, and they drink far less water. Also, the kangaroo is the much-loved national emblem of Australia. It should be easy to protect it.

But it is not that easy. A farmer who sees kangaroos eating the grass he wants for his sheep is still likely to shoot them.

▲ Green, well-watered pastures are ideal for cattle, but they also attract kangaroos in search of food.

FROM DESERT TO PASTURE

In 1845, the explorer Charles Sturt led an expedition through the Outback. Like many explorers, he took no food with him, just a rifle. He found no animals to shoot and abandoned the expedition. Twenty years later, the same areas were well supplied with water and grass, supporting thousands of kangaroos.

Between 1973 and 1981, people thought that kangaroo populations were endangered, so selling their meat and skins was banned in the USA. Since then, kangaroo numbers have risen to a safe level and trade is legal again. Hunters are now licensed to shoot a limited number of kangaroos and sell their skins and meat.

It seems strange that the best way to protect animals is to allow them to be shot. But unless there is some official control on the numbers of kangaroos, farmers will shoot every kangaroo they see, and the large species would be in danger of becoming extinct.

▼ Sheep cannot eat the coarse desert plants, so farmers have had to plant special pastures for them which kangaroos love.

Little rare 'roos

The smaller species of kangaroos are under greater threat than the large ones. Rat kangaroos, for example, are threatened in two ways. They have to compete with rabbits for food and they are hunted by foxes. Two species are already extinct, and three more are endangered. Small grassland kangaroos, such as nail-tail wallabies, are also hunted by foxes and dogs. One species, the crescent nail-tail, is already extinct, and the bridled nail-tail is endangered.

Other small wallabies, potoroos, bettongs and bandicoots, which live in woodlands alongside the grey kangaroos, are under threat as farmers clear their habitat to create new grazing land.

▼ Rufous bettongs are still common in Queensland, north-eastern Australia.

42

EXTINCT AND ENDANGERED

Of the 63 known species of kangaroos, 28 are considered common and safe, 31 are in trouble (listed as endangered, vulnerable or rare), and six are extinct.

The best way to conserve small species would be to set up reserves, but this is not easy. Although Australia is an enormous country, much of it is desert and the land where the small kangaroos live makes good farmland. Predators and land clearance have already done a lot of damage. Still, there are some reserves where the small species of kangaroo are protected.

The main aim of conservation in Australia is to ensure that kangaroos die naturally, rather than being killed by predators brought in from other countries, shooting, loss of habitat or road accidents.

▲ Bridled nail-tail wallabies survive only in a small area of eastern Queensland.

43

Kangaroo Life Cycle

 **1** A baby kangaroo weighs less than 1 gram when it is born. It climbs immediately into its mother's pouch.

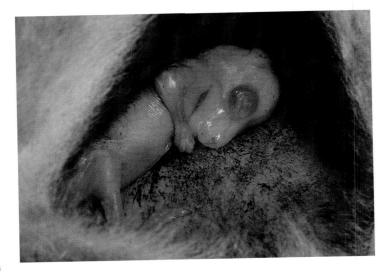

 **2** It completes its development in the pouch, staying there for six to nine months, the first four of them permanently attached to one of the four teats inside.

 **3** After emerging from the pouch, the joey can jump back in for safety and comfort, until it is about 10–12 months old.

 **4** After its mother has stopped it returning to the pouch, the joey stays with the mob in which it was born. Males wander more widely than females.

 **5** Males mature at about four years old, females at 18 months to two years.

 **6** Females usually mate for the first time at three years old, but males must wait until they have grown heavy enough to win fights, usually at five to seven years old.

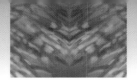

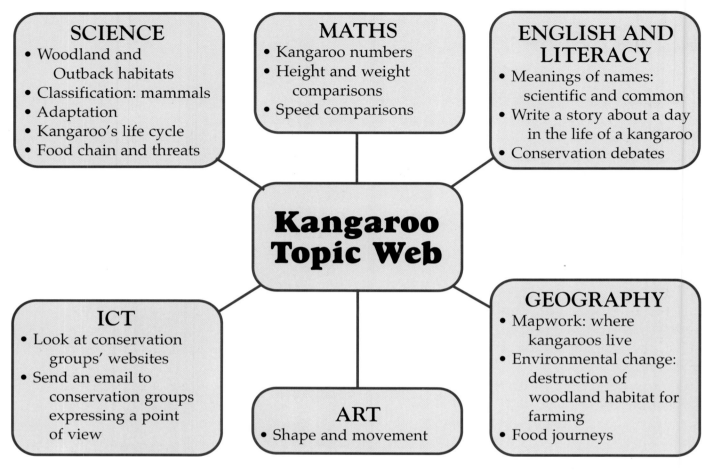

SCIENCE
- Woodland and Outback habitats
- Classification: mammals
- Adaptation
- Kangaroo's life cycle
- Food chain and threats

MATHS
- Kangaroo numbers
- Height and weight comparisons
- Speed comparisons

ENGLISH AND LITERACY
- Meanings of names: scientific and common
- Write a story about a day in the life of a kangaroo
- Conservation debates

Kangaroo Topic Web

ICT
- Look at conservation groups' websites
- Send an email to conservation groups expressing a point of view

ART
- Shape and movement

GEOGRAPHY
- Mapwork: where kangaroos live
- Environmental change: destruction of woodland habitat for farming
- Food journeys

Extension Activities

English
- Debate whether shooting kangaroos should be allowed.
- Find and list collective names for groups of animals, or terms for their young, eg. joey, calf, cub.

Geography
- Trace a world map from an atlas. Show the location of Australia and New Guinea.
- Draw a kangaroo distribution map showing where grey, red, antilopine and tree kangaroos live.

Art
- Make an Australian woodland frieze, showing kangaroos and the other animals that live there.
- Design a kangaroo warning sign for motorists in the Outback.

Science
- Make a chart showing how parts of the kangaroo's body are adapted for certain functions.
- Compare the first months of a kangaroo joey's life with those of another baby animal, such as a lamb.

Glossary

Aborigine One of the first humans to live in Australia.

Bacteria Tiny single-celled creatures.

Carnivorous Meat-eating.

Conservation Keeping and looking after the natural world.

Extinct Died out completely; no longer alive anywhere.

Habitat The place where an animal lives.

Herbivore An animal that only eats plants.

Home range The area that an animal or a family uses to find food.

Omnivorous Able to eat both animals and plants.

Outback The remote inland areas of Australia.

Parasite A creature that feeds from others, often by sucking blood.

Predator An animal that kills and eats other animals.

Proteins Body-building parts of some food.

Reserve An area of land set aside for wild animals, rare plants, etc.

Species A particular sort of animal.

Suckle To provide milk for a baby animal.

Taxidermist Someone who preserves animal skins.

Tendon A strong strip of body tissue that joins a muscle to a bone.

Weaned No longer relying on mother's milk and able to eat solid food.

Further Information

Organizations to Contact

Care for the Wild International
The Granary, Tickfold Farm
Kingsfold, West Sussex
RH12 3SE
Tel: 01306 627900
Website:
www.careforthewild.org.uk

National Kangaroo
Protection Coalition
PO Box 309, Beerwah 4519
Queensland, Australia
Email: austwildlife@iinet.net.au

Books to Read

Kangaroo by Patricia Whitehouse (Heinemann Library, 2002)

The Life Cycle of a Kangaroo by Lisa Trumbauer (Pebble Books/Capstone Press, 2002)

Kangaroos (Zoobooks Series) by Beth Wagner Brust (Wildlife Education Ltd, 2001)

The Kangaroo (Life Cycles) by Sabrina Crewe (Raintree Steck-Vaughn, 1998)

The Secret World of Kangaroos by Malcolm Penny (Raintree Steck-Vaughn, 2002)

Kangaroos (The Untamed World) by Patricia Miller-Schroeder (Raintree Steck-Vaughn, 2002)

Outside and Inside Kangaroos by Sandra Markle (Atheneum Books, 1999)

A Kangaroo Joey Grows Up by Joan Hewett (Carolrhoda, 2001)

Index

Page numbers in **bold** refer to photographs or illustrations.